THE STORY OF BRITAIN

Mick Manning & Brita Granström

Contents

Introducing Britain	2	Plague and Fire	42
From Stone to Bronze	4	The Glorious Revolution	44
Stonehenge	6	The Hanoverians	46
The Iron Age	8	Canals, Roads and Martyrs	48
Roman Britain	10	More Georges	50
Roman Life	12	Georgian Life	52
Anglo~Saxons	14	Industrial Revolution	54
Vikings	16	The Victorians	56
William Conquers!	18	Britain Can Make It!	58
Working for the Normans	20	Victoria's Empire	60
The Plantagenets	22	The Edwardians	62
Lionheart	24	The First World War	64
King John	25	Between the Wars	66
Longshanks	26	The Second World War	68
War and Death	28	The Age of Austerity	70
Cottage Industry	30	The Fab 1960s	72
Henry VIII	32	Hippy to Punk 70s~80s	74
The Elizabethan Age	34	Into the 21st Century	76
Shakespeare and the Globe	36	From Way Back When...	
King James	38	To Here Right Now	78
The English Civil War	40	Index	80

FRANKLIN WATTS

LONDON • SYDNEY

Introducing Britain

Fifty thousand years ago the British Isles weren't islands at all. They were joined to the rest of Europe by a landscape of grassy plains, forests, lakes and rivers that we call 'Doggerland'. Stone Age humans lived there until about 25,000 years ago. Then world temperatures dropped and huge ice sheets slowly covered the land. Humans moved away from the cold to southern Europe, following the animals they hunted, such as wild horses and woolly mammoths.

BRITAIN

DOGGERLAND

We live on wild food: berries, fish and animals.

In the Stone Age humans used stone, bone and antler to make all their tools. They lived in family groups, hunting and also gathering seasonal food such as nuts, berries and fish.

My favourite food is roasted mammoth!

48,000 BC
Humans live in the British landmass and hunt mammoths and wild horses.

23,000 BC
The Ice Age freezes the landscape.
Humans leave Britain and move further south.

Our Ice Age landscape

Giant glaciers, rivers of ice, slid across our landscape in snail-slow-motion. Over thousands of years they bulldozed out valleys, grinding up the debris into gravel and pebbles. Many landscape features we see in Britain today were made during this Ice Age.

Our valleys were gouged out by huge glaciers.

The ice moved slowly downhill and meltwater flowed off its end.

Large rocks were engulfed by ice and slowly ground up by the moving glacier over the course of thousands of years.

Gravel, smoothed pebbles and large boulders were left behind, far from where the glacier picked them up.

Rivers formed.

Lakes were created.

Rising temperatures caused the glacier to melt and retreat.

The end of the Ice Age

About 15,000 years ago, the climate began to grow milder and, over time, the ice began to thaw. As the weather grew warmer, many sorts of animals such as deer and wild horses migrated back across Doggerland followed by human hunters. An endless tangle of trees, 'the wildwood', grew to cover much of the land. As the ice melted it made the sea levels rise; slowly but surely the seas covered Doggerland forever. The British Isles were born!

THE BRITISH ISLES

English Channel

Britain is now an island! Our story has begun.

13,000 BC
The ice begins to thaw.
Doggerland slowly begins to flood.

6,000 BC
Britain is now an island.

From Stone to Bronze

For thousands of years life went on unchanged until about 6,500 years ago when a new idea reached the hunter-gatherers in Britain – farming. Why not keep animals such as goats and pigs and breed them for milk or meat? Why not grow some plants yourself instead of foraging for them? But this farming revolution didn't happen overnight. It took hundreds, perhaps thousands of years to spread right across Britain. Even then, farmers did some hunting and gathering to add to their homegrown food supply.

Pigs and goats help us to clear the wildwood.

The farmers' year followed the seasons: ploughing, planting and harvesting crops; rearing and slaughtering farm animals. Farmers worshipped gods and goddesses they hoped would bless this back-breaking work: moon goddesses, sun gods, weather gods and fertility gods. They also started to build chambered tombs to bury their dead.

4,500 BC
Neolithic farmers.
Farming comes to Britain.

4,000 BC
People start firing clay pots in an oven to make them stronger.

3,000 BC
Monuments such as
Stonehenge begin to be built.

4

During the Stone Age areas of wildwood were cleared using flint axes, fire, wooden ploughs and perhaps pigs to snuffle-out the stumps and roots.

We decorate our pots with patterns.

Timber!

Metalwork

Our ancestors used tools made of wood, flint and bone until about 4,500 years ago when a new discovery, metalworking, came to Britain. People used copper at first but it was too soft to be much use and gradually another technique was perfected: mixing molten copper and tin together to make a much tougher metal called bronze.

About 6,000 years ago people started firing clay pots. Pot fragments tell us a lot about our ancestors. We know new people were arriving in Britain at the start of the Bronze Age because they brought a new style of pot – we call them the 'Beaker People'.

Bronze tools and weapons were much stronger than copper and could have much sharper cutting edges.

This mould is for an axe-head.

During the Bronze Age another revolution took place. People learned how to spin and weave woollen cloth for clothing, cloaks and blankets.

2,500 BC
The Beaker People arriving in Britain from mainland Europe.

2,000 BC
People in Britain are now making bronze tools and weapons.

1,500 BC
Stonehenge is completed at about this time.

5

A boy's day at Stonehenge

1. Wolf and his dad are helping to build Stonehenge. Each massive stone is so heavy it takes dozens of people using rollers and ropes to drag it into position. The bluestones have come from as far away as the Welsh mountains. The huge Sarsens are from the Marlborough Downs.

2. Wolf's job is to dig pits for the stones to help them stand up. They need to be deep and square — and packed down hard. It's back-breaking work. But hundreds of people are helping to build this amazing monument.

3. Wolf's dad is one of a team dragging the huge Sarsen stones into place. Expert stonemasons have hammered and carved joints — bumps and holes so the stones fit snugly together.

4. Slowly but surely they lever each lintel stone higher and higher by placing timbers underneath it. Then they push, shove and slide it into position on top of a pair of upright stones.

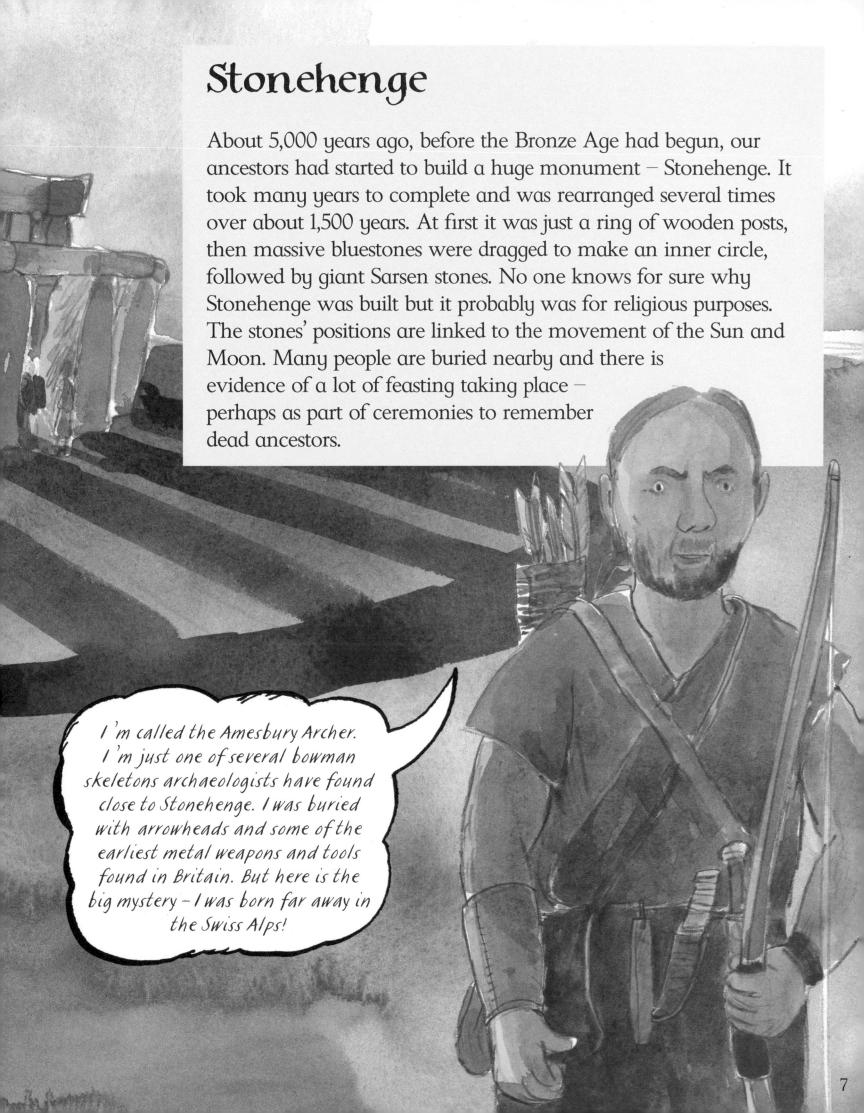

Stonehenge

About 5,000 years ago, before the Bronze Age had begun, our ancestors had started to build a huge monument – Stonehenge. It took many years to complete and was rearranged several times over about 1,500 years. At first it was just a ring of wooden posts, then massive bluestones were dragged to make an inner circle, followed by giant Sarsen stones. No one knows for sure why Stonehenge was built but it probably was for religious purposes. The stones' positions are linked to the movement of the Sun and Moon. Many people are buried nearby and there is evidence of a lot of feasting taking place – perhaps as part of ceremonies to remember dead ancestors.

I'm called the Amesbury Archer. I'm just one of several bowman skeletons archaeologists have found close to Stonehenge. I was buried with arrowheads and some of the earliest metal weapons and tools found in Britain. But here is the big mystery – I was born far away in the Swiss Alps!

The Iron Age

About 1,000 years after Stonehenge was finished, the Celts began crossing the sea to Britain. They came from central Europe and had already settled in France and Spain. They lived in settlements led by chieftains that belonged to a larger regional tribe ruled by a king and their royal family. By this time humans had discovered iron and the skills of iron-working. It was a huge improvement for tools and weapons because iron was much stronger than bronze.

A Celtic roundhouse was made using local materials such as wattle (split branches woven together) and daub (mud and animal dung mixed together). It could be up to 12 metres high and 13 metres across, providing a large, warm home.

I am making flour.

Iron was extracted from iron ore in fiery furnaces. It was hammered into sharp-edged axes, swords and farming tools.

Another invention, quern stones, meant it became easier to grind grain and bake bread. Until then, most grains had been eaten as a sort of porridge.

800 BC	700-500 BC	600 BC
Start of the period known as the British Iron Age.	Iron-working skills spread across Britain.	People begin to build Maiden Castle, a hill fort in Dorset.

British Celtic tribes built hill forts – large, defensive structures with ditches and ring fences often placed on high ground for safety. Sometimes they built their own houses inside.

The Celts

Celtic society included warriors, Druids (Celtic holy men), poet-storytellers, craftsmen and healers. Warriors would gather around their log fires and listen to stories about superhuman heroes such as Finn McCool. But Celtic life was about to change dramatically – the Romans were coming...

Our clothes are woven from brightly dyed cloth not unlike the traditional cloth you know as 'tartan'.

We warriors grow long moustaches and tattoo ourselves with blue dye. Some warriors spike their hair using lime whitewash.

330 BC
A Greek merchant writes about his travels around Britain.

200 BC
Celtic metalwork skills reach ever-higher levels.

100 BC
First building of stone towers called 'brochs' in Scotland.

9

Roman Britain

The Romans came from what is now Italy, and they built an empire that stretched from Turkey across most of Europe. Although the Roman general Julius Caesar had attacked Britain in 55 and 56 BC, it wasn't until AD 43 that the Romans invaded in force. After fierce fighting, the Celtic leader Caratacus was captured and the powerful Druid priests were hunted down and killed; Britain was conquered.

SCOTLAND
(Caledonia)

Antonine Wall

Hadrian's Wall

York

Anglesey
(Druids defeated here)

Ermine Street

Boudica's Iceni Tribe

Watling Street

St Albans

Bath

Colchester

London

Fosse Way

We nicknamed the Britons Brittunculi meaning 'Nasty little Brits'. But many Brits soon accepted our way of life. Some have even joined the Roman army.

Celtic chariot with blades on the wheels

Boudica's Revolt

It didn't all go the Romans' way. In AD 60, Boudica, queen of the Iceni tribe, raised a rebellion. Her followers massacred the people of Colchester, St Albans and London before she was finally defeated.

55/56 BC	AD 43	AD 60
First attacks on Britain by Julius Caesar.	The Roman Emperor Claudius invades Britain.	Boudica leads a bloody revolt but is defeated by the Roman army.

The Roman army was made up of legions of about 6,000 soldiers, plus cavalry and auxiliary units (men recruited from other countries). Each legion was divided into centuries – platoons of 80 men, each led by an officer called a centurion.

The Romans built straight, paved roads for easier, faster marching to trouble spots. Their roads were so well made that stretches of many modern-day roads still sit on top of them.

HALT!

Centurion

Standard bearer

Trumpeter

Short stabbing sword

Shield

Hadrian's Wall

The Romans tried unsuccessfully to conquer Scotland. To protect their empire and show their power, they built Hadrian's Wall, stretching from Newcastle to Carlisle. In AD 140 the Romans built the Antonine Wall, where Glasgow is today. However, only 23 years later, they abandoned it for good.

It's colder than Germany!

I'm missing sunny Spain!

AD 122
Hadrian's Wall is built.

AD 140
Antonine Wall is built.

AD 163
Romans pull out of Scotland for good.

Roman Life

Rome brought a new way of life to Britain – town life – building the first British towns, such as London (Londinium) and Bath (Aquae Sulis). Mixed populations of Britons and Romans (often retired soldiers) we call Romano-Britons moved in. These Britons became 'civilised' (from the Latin word *civis*, meaning someone who lives in a town) and enjoyed shops, bars and bathhouses as citizens of the Roman Empire.

A Romano-British boy's day

1. Today is Saturn's day and Cato is visiting the temple. Roman gods are led by Jupiter and Juno, followed by Saturn, god of harvest and plenty, Venus, goddess of love, Apollo, god of the Sun, and Neptune, god of the sea.

2. After that Cato has lessons in reading, writing, maths and fighting. Only boys from well-off families can afford this education while girls stay at home to learn cookery and needlework.

3. Cato's father is a rich merchant and they are holding a feast tonight with some of the foods the Romans introduced into Britain, such as cabbages, pheasants, rabbits, snails cooked in butter and baked dormice. Romans eat lying down.

4. After the feast they visit the local amphitheatre to watch gladiators fight — but not to the death. These two are famous and far too valuable to be allowed to kill each other! The Romans have built amphitheatres all over Britain, including: Colchester, St Albans, Melrose and London.

Romans loved mosaic floors – pictures made of tiny coloured tiles. This head of a pagan god was found at Verulamium – a place we now call St Albans, after the first British Christian martyr. Alban was a Romano-Briton living in Verulamium who gave shelter to a Christian priest at a time when Christians were persecuted by the Romans. When soldiers came to arrest the priest, Alban gave himself up in the priest's place and was beheaded. Other mosaics such as those excavated at Lullingstone Villa in Kent show early evidence of Christians in Britain.

Anglo~Saxons

In the early 5th Century the Roman army abandoned Britain to defend their capital from invading Germanic tribes. Left alone, Romano-British rulers hired warrior-bands from Northern Europe to defend them. But these warriors began to take land instead, encouraging more Angle, Jute and Saxon settlers to arrive. These Anglo-Saxons took over, developing well-organised, cultured warrior kingdoms that would last for hundreds of years.

Settling down

These warrior-bands were looking to settle down and farm, bringing their families from northern Germany, the Netherlands and Denmark. The Angles took land in the north and east, while the Saxons and the Jutes settled to the south of them. By AD 600 the Anglo-Saxons controlled 'Angle-land' – England. Some Celts retreated west to Wales and Cornwall, others made peace.

England was divided into many Anglo-Saxon kingdoms: East Anglia, Sussex, Wessex, Northumbria and Mercia. Their kings often fought each other for power and land.

The legendary King Arthur may be based on a Romano-British leader who fought against the early Anglo-Saxon invaders.

Get yourself back to Denmark.

The Anglo-Saxons brought a new language with them, which evolved into the English we speak today. But the Celtic language survived as Welsh, Cornish and Gaelic.

AD 400-500	600	672
Romans leave Britain. Angles, Jutes and Saxons begin to settle.	Anglo-Saxons ruling 'Angle-land' divided into many small kingdoms.	Birth of the historian Bede, known as 'the Venerable'.

Beowulf

1. One of the great poems of Anglo-Saxon writing is 'Beowulf'. It was written down in Britain around the 8th century but is a much older, word-of-mouth 'campfire' story from the Saxon homeland.

2. Beowulf is the hero of the epic, who fights dragons and monsters. The most famous part of the story is where Beowulf battles with the man-eating monster Grendel.

3. Then worse still, he takes on the monster's mother... The original Beowulf story was pagan but the Anglo-Saxon version was written from a Christian viewpoint.

Religion

The early Anglo-Saxons believed in pagan gods such as Wodin. But over time, many became Christians. Christian monasteries were built by Irish monks on Iona in Scotland and later, Lindisfarne in Northumbria. Missionaries came from the Pope in Rome to the south of England, too. Anglo-Saxon monks produced beautifully illustrated Bible texts such as the *Lindisfarne Gospels*.

One of the most famous Saxon discoveries is the Sutton Hoo ship burial - possibly the grave of the East Anglian King Raedwald. Dating from the 600s, it contained a treasure hoard, including this amazing warrior helmet, buried inside a long boat.

An Anglo-Saxon monk called Bede wrote a famous book called **History of the English Church and People** – the first history of Britain!

Many of England's village churches were first built by the Anglo-Saxons.

Our peaceful Christian monasteries were soon to be attacked - from the fury of the Northmen deliver us, Oh Lord!

700
The *Lindisfarne Gospels* illustrated in Northumbria.

757-796
King Offa of Mercia rules central England and builds Offa's Dyke.

793
Vikings raid Lindisfarne's monastery.

Vikings

The Vikings originally came from Norway (Norsemen), Denmark and Sweden (Danes). In 793 Viking raiders began the plunder of English monasteries with a devastating attack on Lindisfarne. Eventually a large Viking force known as 'The Great Army' invaded Britain in 865, looking for plunder, but also for land to settle and in which to live peacefully.

SCOTLAND

IRELAND

Dublin

Northumbria
York

DANELAW

Mercia

East Anglia

WESSEX

My name is Ivar the Boneless.

We've come to start a new life in England.

Vikings had a fearsome reputation as warriors and yet Viking women, unlike Saxon women, had a lot of freedom. They could own property, divorce their husbands and run respectable businesses.

865	866	870-874
The Viking Great Army invades Britain.	The Vikings capture York. It will become their capital.	Vikings take over the Saxon kingdoms of East Anglia and Mercia.

The Danelaw

Years of fighting followed as Vikings made bases in Scotland, Ireland and large areas of England. But when they were finally defeated in battle by King Alfred, the ruler of Wessex, the Vikings signed a peace treaty. This divided England between the Vikings and the Anglo-Saxons and was called 'The Danelaw'. Many Vikings settled down, intermarrying with local Anglo-Saxons in the north and east. They became farmers, craftsmen and traders; historians call the descendants of these mixed settlers 'Anglo-Scandinavians'.

Jorvik (modern York) became the Viking capital and a world-famous centre of trade.

Look at the wolf skins, Mum!

England united?

Power struggles continued but in 937 the Anglo-Saxon King Aethelstan became the first king of the whole of England. Much later, Canute became the first Christian Viking king of England. The parable of him proving he was not all-powerful (by unsuccessfully commanding the tide not to rise) is still told today. Canute was succeeded by two of his sons, then Edward the Confessor, an Anglo-Saxon, came to the throne of England.

Traces of Vikings and Saxons

From this time the descriptions 'English', 'Scottish' and 'Irish' include people of Viking descent. Over 3000 words in the English language alone have Scandinavian roots.

Viking place-name endings include *gate*, *by* and *ness*.

Saxon place-name endings include *ton*, *bury* and *wich*.

Everyday Viking words include husband, window, egg and knife.

Everyday Saxon words include man, house, apple and nail.

The Vikings soon converted to Christianity but the names of their old gods (and the Saxons') gave us days of the week such as:

Tuesday from Tyr, god of bravery;

Wednesday from Odin, god of wisdom, victory and death;

Thursday from Thor, the thunder god;

Friday from Frey (pronounced 'Fry' by the Danes), the god of farmers, fertility and business.

I command you, waves, not to wet my feet!

877
King Alfred of Wessex defeats the Vikings in battle.

884
The Danelaw is established after many more battles.

1016-1035
The rule of King Canute, who becomes a Christian.

William Conquers!

I crown you King Harold.

In 1066 when King Edward the Confessor died, the English nobles chose Harold Godwinson, Earl of Wessex, to be King of England. With a Viking princess as his mother, and a Saxon earl for a father, Harold was a popular choice for the English throne. But Duke William of Normandy in France had other ideas. He insisted he had been promised the throne and even claimed that Earl Harold had sworn to support him . . .

Stamford Bridge

ENGLAND

London

Hastings

Normandy

FRANCE

The Battle of Hastings

King Harold had problems: first the King of Norway and Harold's own brother attacked him in the north. Harold marched his army to York and defeated them at the Battle of Stamford Bridge. Yet even as the English celebrated victory, news came that the Norman army had landed on the south coast. Harold marched his weary army south again to a place called Hastings. He found a strong hill-top position to fight from but the Normans tricked the English into an attack down the hill. Harold was killed alongside his bodyguards. William had conquered.

We pretended to run away - and the English chased us, leaving the safety of the hill. Then our cavalry charged...

Helmet

Chainmail

Charge!

Shield

1042-1066
Edward 'the Confessor' rules England.

25 September 1066
Battle of Stamford Bridge. The English defeat the Norse.

14 October 1066
The Battle of Hastings. The Normans defeat the English.

The harrowing of the north

Legends grew around freedom fighters such as Cambridgeshire's Hereward the Wake but when rebels overthrew the Norman garrison in York, the Normans laid waste to the region, massacring the people and destroying crops and water supplies. English resistance was crushed but plenty of battles and skirmishes continued between the Normans and the Scots and the Welsh.

Burn the lot!

William began to build castles and cathedrals – one of the first buildings was the Tower of London built using stone specially brought from France.

The Bayeaux Tapestry tells the story of the Battle of Hastings in pictures. It was made by skilful English embroiderers like me!

The Domesday Book

William rewarded his Norman barons by giving them the defeated English nobles' land and property. He ordered a survey of his kingdom (which also included parts of South Wales) so he could make the English pay heavy taxes. This survey, called the 'Domesday Book', listed the names and possessions of many English people. It survives to this day.

Next!

I have four ducks, two pigs and three geese.

25 December 1066	1070-72	1086
William is crowned King of England at Westminster Abbey.	The revolt of Hereward the Wake and the harrowing of the north.	The Domesday Book survey is completed.

Working for the Normans

In many areas, Norman lords and knights used the 'open-field' system, dividing their farmland into hundreds of narrow strips. The peasants who lived on that land were required to work on it for their lord. In return they were allowed to farm some field strips for themselves and also to use 'common land' on their lord's manor; woodland for firewood and pasture to graze their animals. All peasants had to swear an oath of loyalty to their Norman lords. Freemen such as smallholders had to pay rents to and tithes (shares of any produce) to their lords and the Church, as well as taxes to the king. For most, life under the Normans was backbreaking, while the barons, knights and bishops grew richer.

All we do is work, work, work for our Norman masters!

I'm fed up with paying taxes to our lords and tithes to our priests!

Squire to knight

I'll be a knight one day.

Only sons of noblemen could become knights. They became apprenticed to a knight as a squire, often moving away from home to live with their master until they qualified as a knight themselves. It was hard work but a squire had a comfortable life compared to a peasant.

The feudal system

To control the conquered population, the Normans took away all land from the Anglo-Saxon lords and gave it to powerful Normans instead. They governed through a complex web of relationships, often called the feudal system, which worked something like this:

The Royal family

The King owned all the land. He gave some land to trusted supporters in exchange for their help in ruling the country and raising toops if necessary.

Norman lords

In turn, these powerful barons, earls and bishops (the church was given huge amounts of land) gave some of their land to knights. The knights promised to support them, if needed, by fighting and governing the land.

Knights

Knights maintained justice in their local area. Each knight allowed peasants to live on the land in exchange for working the land and paying taxes and tithes – a share of the harvest.

Stop moaning, you two. At least we'll have a feast once we've got the harvest in.

Peasants

Below the knights and landowners were the peasants, who worked the land or were craftsmen such as blacksmiths and carpenters. Peasants had little power and some were desperately poor. They had to do what their overlords said to survive.

The Plantagenets

William the Conqueror died in 1087 and his son William 'Rufus' now ruled England while his brother Robert ruled France. Then in 1100 William Rufus was accidentally killed by an arrow while hunting in the New Forest and another brother Henry was quickly crowned king. Henry I then went to war, defeating his brother Robert in France. When Henry died in 1135 his daughter, Matilda and his nephew Stephen fought for power. . . Finally Matilda's son became the first Plantagenet king: Henry II.

Murder in the cathedral

I cannot agree!

1. In 1162 Henry II persuaded his old friend Thomas Becket to be Archbishop of Canterbury, but then he and Henry disagreed over religion.

Will no one rid me of this turbulent priest?

2. Henry and Thomas had lots of rows. One day, Henry was heard to shout out something like: 'Will no one rid me of this turbulent priest?'

3. Upon hearing this, four of his knights went into Canterbury Cathedral and stabbed Archbishop Becket to death!

4. The whole of Europe was horrified by the murder and Henry was made to beg for forgiveness at Thomas's tomb.

God forgive me.

5. Becket became an instant martyr and was soon made a saint. People began to go on pilgrimages to Canterbury to visit his tomb.

1100	1100	1135
Henry seizes the English throne.	Henry I marries Matilda, daughter of Malcolm III of Scotland.	Henry I dies and his daughter and nephew fight for power.

Conquering Ireland

Around 1169, King Henry allowed knights from England to support the King of Leinster in Ireland. More knights went the following year led by the Earl of Pembroke, Richard de Clare, also known as 'Strongbow', who then married the Irish king's daughter. This made King Henry nervous, so he landed his own army and forced Strongbow to pledge his loyalty. Later, many English barons carved out their own small kingdoms in Ireland.

A strong king

Henry brought order back to England after the troubled years of Stephen and Matilda. He introduced a fairer legal system and trial by jury.

Henry made sure judges travelled around the country hearing cases throughout the kingdom rather than just in London.

I am Strongbow. I love Ireland and when I die I shall be buried in Dublin.

I am Queen Eleanor of Aquitaine, Henry's wife. He and I fell out - and three of our sons took my side. When Henry died he was at war with his own son, Richard the Lionheart.

1154	1173	1183
Henry II, grandson of Henry I, is crowned King of England.	Henry's eldest son, 'Young Henry', leads a rebellion against his father.	Young Henry is killed in a revolt. Richard is now heir to the throne.

Lionheart

When Richard I was king he spent much of his life away from England, either governing his lands in France or taking part in the Crusades. The Crusades were a series of bloody wars against the Seljuk Turks, the Muslim warriors who in 1187 stopped Christian pilgrims from visiting Jerusalem in the Holy Land. The Pope promised that God would pardon every knight's sins if they went on a crusade to win back Jerusalem for the Christians. King Richard led the Third Crusade.

Christians believed they could be forgiven for any sins by making pilgrimages to holy places. Many visited the grave of Saint Thomas Becket in Canterbury. Others journeyed as far as the Holy Land – a reason that started the Crusades.

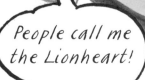

People call me the Lionheart!

Saladin was said to be a great leader who ruled wisely and fairly.

To Jerusalem

Crusaders were religious but some went on crusades for other reasons too – in search of power and land or to have an adventure. Faced by the skilful forces of the Muslim leader Saladin, the crusaders failed to capture Jerusalem. Eventually, in 1192, Richard made a treaty with the Turks allowing pilgrims to visit in peace.

1187	1189	1190
Saladin takes Jerusalem, held by the Christians since 1099.	Henry II dies and his son Richard I becomes king.	Richard I leaves England to lead the Third Crusade.

King John

John, Richard's younger brother, had plotted to take the throne, but then in 1199 Richard died and John became king anyway. King John quickly lost the crown's lands in France so he raised taxes to fund a war to win them back. The angry English nobles rebelled against him and forced King John to sign an agreement to limit his power. This was called Magna Carta which means 'the great agreement'.

I steal from the rich and give to the poor.

This is the age of the legendary Robin Hood, who hid out with his gang of outlaws, his 'merry men', in the ancient wildwood that then still stretched between Sheffield and Nottingham.

Now our king must listen to us!

Sign here, Your Majesty!

Just you wait and see...

Magna Carta was signed in a 'meeting meadow' at Runnymede on the River Thames.

Magna Carta

Magna Carta was a document drawn up to try to limit the king's power, for example his right to take people's land. Although King John actually ignored these rules, future kings upheld Magna Carta and it became an important part of English law.

1192-94
Richard held captive in Europe. He returns to England after a ransom is paid.

1199
Richard dies and his brother John becomes king.

1215
King John signs Magna Carta.

Longshanks

King John died in 1216 and was succeeded by his son Henry III. Henry reigned for 56 years but struggled to keep power. He was helped by his strong, war-like son Edward Longshanks, another crusader, who became king in 1272. Edward ruled fairly but often cruelly, particularly when he invaded Wales and Scotland. Many imposing castles were built in Wales and filled with soldiers to control the local people.

I'm so tall they call me Longshanks!

Many of Edward's Welsh castles still stand today, such as Conwy, Harlech and Caernarfon; monuments to the king's power and ruthlessness.

Taking on Wales

After years of trying to conquer Gwynedd (North Wales) King Edward's army (over half were from other parts of Wales) defeated Welsh leader Llywelyn ap Gruffydd and his forces. By 1277 Edward had started the English colonisation of Wales, creating new towns such as Aberystwyth. Some Welsh peasants were forced to leave their land, which was given to English peasants. War broke out again in 1282 when Llywelyn and his brother Dafydd rebelled. Eventually Llywelyn was killed in battle and his brother executed. In 1301, Edward proclaimed his eldest son Prince of Wales – a title still given to the heir to the British throne today.

Victory is ours!

1216	1264	1265
Nine-year-old Henry III becomes king.	Start of Second Barons' War. Simon de Montfort wins control of England.	Edward defeats de Montfort at Evesham. Henry back in full power by 1267.

Scotland

The English king had a lot of influence in Scotland and in 1292 Edward chose John Balliol to be the Scots' king at a meeting in the castle at Berwick upon Tweed. But later, when Edward demanded Scotland send soldiers to help in his war against France, Scotland made allies of the French instead. In 1296, they attacked the English border town of Carlisle, so Edward invaded Scotland. The Scots fought back but, in 1305, their leader William Wallace was captured and executed.

Never surrender!

Wallace was a fierce fighter.

I must keep trying...

Legend tells of Robert the Bruce hiding in a cave and watching a spider try again and again to spin a web. This inspired him to victory and gave us the motto: 'If at first you don't succeed, try, try again!'

Robert the Bruce, King of the Scots, eventually led the Scots to victory at the Battle of Bannockburn in 1314 where he defeated Edward II. He was recognised as king of an independent Scotland. An official peace treaty was signed in 1327.

The Battle of Bannockburn near Stirling was a great victory for the Scottish.

The English are defeated.

The Bruce has led the Scots to victory!

1272	1282	1306	1307	1314
Edward I becomes king.	Wales is now fully under English rule.	Robert the Bruce crowned King of the Scots.	Edward II becomes king.	Scots win the Battle of Bannockburn.

War and Death

Between 1337 and 1485 two wars kept England very busy. First they fought the French and then they fought each other . . .

The Hundred Years' War

This series of battles in France was a power struggle over French land. King Edward III defeated the French at the bloody battles of Crécy and Poitiers, but the wars continued until Henry V's famous victory at Agincourt in 1415. Here, outnumbered by French knights on horseback, Henry used his elite English and Welsh longbow-men. Up to 1,000 arrows a second rained down on the charging French cavalry, piercing armour, flesh and bone. Henry won a huge victory, but that wasn't the end. Inspired by the famous Joan of Arc, the French eventually drove the English (by then led by Henry V's son Henry VI) out of France in 1453.

Grip the arrow with your first two fingers...

Like this?

English and Welsh bowmen had to train from about 15 to develop the huge strength needed to fire a longbow. Every village had its own 'butts', a firing range where all men had to attend regular target practice by law.

A plague epidemic reached Britain in 1348 when black rats carrying infected fleas arrived on ships from Europe. It was called the 'Black Death', after the black swellings that appeared in the victims' armpits. These were followed by fever, vomiting – and death. Over half the population of Britain died.

1327	1337-1453	1348
Edward II is murdered. His son becomes Edward III.	The Hundred Years' War. England has five different kings during this period.	The Black Death reaches Britain. Over half the population dies.

Wars of the Roses

Not long after the end of the Hundred Years War, Henry VI was declared insane and supporters of two rival branches of the Plantagenet family – the House of York (whose symbol was the white rose) and the House of Lancaster (the red rose) – began a long struggle for the crown.

The throne see-sawed between both sides as battles were won and lost. But when the last Plantagenet king Richard III was defeated and killed at the Battle of Bosworth in 1485, the Lancastrian leader, Henry Tudor, became king.

I am surrounded...

Richard has lost his horse. Come on, lads, kill him!

Look he has a crown. He must be King Richard!

I am Richard III, the last Plantagenet king.

Henry was crowned at Bosworth with the crown Richard had worn into battle. Richard's naked body was paraded to Leicester and buried simply. In 2012 a skeleton was discovered under a car park there and, after careful study, experts announced they had found the body of King Richard III, the last king of England to die in battle.

I am Henry Tudor and I began a new dynasty.

| 1381 | 1387-1400 | 1455-85 | 1476 |
| Richard II defeats the Peasants' Revolt. | Chaucer writes *The Canterbury Tales*. | The Wars of the Roses. They end with Henry Tudor becoming king. | Caxton prints the first book in England. |

29

City and town guilds

In the 14th century craftsmen and merchants formed trade guilds to protect their reputations and maintain standards. Each guild held the rights in a town to control the supply and sale of their type of trade.

Craftsmen and traders

Guilds included wool merchants, weavers, stonemasons, brick layers, carpenters, gold and silversmiths, wine merchants and shopkeepers. In many cases guild members also made important decisions about their town's development. Traces of this role exist today in the town halls, run by local officials such as mayors and sheriffs.

Lord Mayor

Dick Whittington (about 1350-1423) was a cloth merchant who became a master of his guild and eventually Lord Mayor of London. He is remembered in the famous pantomime with his clever cat.

Shall I go back to London?

Qualifications

Guilds introduced approved stages of qualification: apprentice, then craftsman, journeyman, master and grand master. Only a few people reached the highest level of skill.

Mystery plays

Guilds also performed mystery plays on feast days. These were based on the Bible: the Tailors might tell the story of Noah's Ark or the Carpenters perform the story of shepherds visiting the baby Jesus. People loved them.

At a joust two knights charged at each other with a lance, trying to unhorse their opponent in front of crowds of spectators. Henry VIII (meet him on the next page) was keen on jousting!

Cottage Industry

After the Black Death, the pageantry and romance of jousting knights remained a popular spectacle for rich and poor. But times were changing because there were fewer people to work the land. In 1381 there was a peasants' revolt against new taxes and poor living conditions. Many landowners started to profit from keeping huge flocks of sheep, and more and more people moved to the growing towns to look for work. Meanwhile, clever merchants set up networks of home-based workers who spun and wove the wool from the sheep into cloth. This cottage industry would last for hundreds of years.

Geoffrey Chaucer

Geoffrey Chaucer was a royal diplomat and a writer. His most famous work, *The Canterbury Tales*, uses everyday English and everyday people as his models, as well as lots of knights and ladies.

I'm called 'the father of English literature'.

William Caxton

Caxton brought the printing press to Britain from Europe. By inking up movable type and using a press Caxton mass-produced books in English. Before this books were hand-written, expensive and mainly in Latin. Caxton's books included Chaucer's *Canterbury Tales* and Malory's *Tales of King Arthur*.

Henry VIII

King Henry (the second son of Henry VII) is famous for marrying six times because he desperately wanted a son to be the next Tudor king. He fell out with the Catholics and the Pope in Rome because they wouldn't let him divorce his first wife, Catherine. To get what he wanted he made himself head of a new Church of England and gave himself a divorce. Henry ruled for 38 years and raised three children by different wives. His son, Edward, ruled after him.

1503	1509	1533
Henry VII's daughter Margaret marries James IV of Scotland.	Henry VIII becomes King of England.	Henry divorces Catherine of Aragon and marries Anne Boleyn.

The English Reformation

The Reformation that Henry brought to England had begun in Europe, with preachers like Martin Luther suggesting a new, simpler way of Christian worship, where people used their own language, not Latin as the Roman Catholics did. Supported by Archbishop Thomas Cranmer and the Lord Chancellor, Thomas Cromwell, Henry set about reforming the English Church, ordering services to be given in English and the dissolution (closing down) of Roman Catholic monasteries.

Henry seized all the monasteries' valuables and lands for himself, leaving many in ruins and their monks and nuns homeless or in prison.

They are even taking the lead off the roof!

Thomas Cromwell

The son of a blacksmith, Thomas Cromwell became Henry VIII's right-hand man. He was Secretary of State, Lord Chancellor, Lord Privy Seal, Lord Chamberlain and governor of the Isle of Wight – all at the same time! Cromwell was one of the strongest supporters of the Reformation and helped Henry divorce, execute and re-marry. But, after arranging a bad marriage to Anne of Cleves, he fell out with King Henry and was himself executed in 1540.

Edward ~ the boy king

On Henry's death his son, Edward VI, ruled for six years. He was a devout Protestant and, with the help of Archbishop Cranmer, he strengthened the Church of England until his own death aged only 15. Edward left the throne to his 16-year-old cousin, Lady Jane Grey, hoping this tactic would prevent his Catholic half-sister Mary from becoming queen.

I am Edward. Under my rule the Book of Common Prayer was published. It is still used in Anglican churches.

1534	1536	1540-43	1547
Church of England breaks from the Roman Catholic Church.	Anne beheaded. Henry marries Jane Seymour.	Henry marries again: Cleves (1540), Howard (1540) and Parr (1543).	Edward VI becomes king. 33

The Elizabethan Age

Jane would be queen for only nine days – and was later executed for treason. Mary took the throne with little resistance and quickly restored the Catholic religion, which many people welcomed. But her marriage to Prince (later King) Philip of Spain and the burning of hundreds of Protestants at the stake were less popular. She would become known as 'Bloody Mary'. Five years later she died and her half-sister Elizabeth became queen.

The Elizabethan Age was a time of explorers such as Francis Drake who sailed around the world in his ship the **Golden Hind**. He also plundered Spanish treasure ships laden with gold stolen from the conquered Inca and Aztec nations in South America.

'I know I have the body of a weak and feeble woman; but I have the heart and stomach of a king, and of a king of England too...'

Drake arrived back from his travels in Plymouth in 1580 with a huge fortune. He wisely shared it with Queen Elizabeth and was knighted on board his ship.

1553
Lady Jane Grey briefly reigns, then Mary takes the throne.

1556
Thomas Cranmer is burnt at the stake.

1558
Elizabeth I becomes Queen of England.

1564
William Shakespeare is born.

The Spanish Armada

Queen Elizabeth returned her kingdom to the Protestant religion. This enraged the Pope in Rome. Catholic monarchs made threats, especially King Philip of Spain, who also blamed Elizabeth for encouraging her sea captains to raid his treasure ships. In 1588, Spain sent a fleet of warships to invade England. Although smaller, the English ships were more manoeuvrable and had skilful captains, such as Sir Francis Drake. A sea battle took place in the English Channel. The English used fireships to break up the Armada then chased it up the east coast. The Spanish tried to escape by sailing around the British Isles but about 50 Spanish ships were either sunk or shipwrecked.

Another explorer, Sir Walter Raleigh, founded the first British colony in America. He brought back tobacco and potatoes to England.

Mary Queen of Scots

Mary Stuart, Elizabeth's cousin, was a Catholic and her supporters believed she should replace Elizabeth. Mary had been brought up in France but, on returning to rule Scotland, she found a strongly Protestant country and she was forced to seek protection from her cousin in England. With no heir and plenty of Catholic rebels in England, Elizabeth kept Mary under guard in various country houses for 20 years until Mary became caught up in plots to take Elizabeth's throne. She was beheaded at Fotheringhay Castle in 1587 and this royal execution shocked Europe.

My son James is King of Scotland and he will become King of England and Wales too when Elizabeth dies!

1587
Mary Queen of Scots is executed. Her son becomes James VI of Scotland.

1588
The Spanish Armada is defeated.

1600
The East India Company is set up to trade with India and the Far East.

Shakespeare and the Globe

The Elizabethan Age saw the Protestant Church re-established with some Catholics now burnt at the stake. It was also a later part of the Renaissance, an outburst of artistic creativity that spread across the whole of Europe. In Britain musicians such as Thomas Tallis composed amazing new choral music and writers such as Christopher Marlowe and William Shakespeare drew huge audiences to their plays, attracting both rich and poor alike to the newly built theatres. Queen Elizabeth herself saw Shakespeare perform at least twice at her Royal Palace in Greenwich.

I'm William Shakespeare, the son of a glove maker in Stratford-upon-Avon, but I will become the most famous writer in the world. Just look at all these phrases people use - I wrote them down first in my plays.

He's a laughing stock!

My only love sprung from my only hate!

That dress has seen better days.

What the Dickens!

The boy Shakespeare

WOW!

Alas, poor Yorick!

1. As a boy William Shakespeare loved watching the local mystery plays. Troupes of actors also visited Stratford-upon-Avon.

2. Although we don't know everything about his life we can guess Will joined a troupe of actors and became an apprentice helping out backstage.

*3. He became our greatest writer, famous for his plays such as **Romeo and Juliet**, **Hamlet** and **A Midsummer Night's Dream**.*

Dead as a doornail.

It's a fool's paradise.

He is a tower of strength.

Did my heart love until now?

The game is up...

She is tongue-tied.

What an eyesore!

They're in a pickle!

Welcome to the Globe! It is a noisy, stinky theatre but full of people keen to laugh and cry.

Send him packing!

King James

Elizabeth ruled until she was 69 years old - a great age in those days. Before she died she named Mary Stuart's son (who was by then King James VI of Scotland) as the next king of England, Wales and Ireland. James was the first of the Stuart family to rule England but he was already an experienced Scottish ruler. He was a Protestant king with very strong views about his royal power; in fact he believed his right to rule was given to him by God . . .

The Gunpowder Plot

1. In 1605, a group of English Catholics decided to try and blow up the Houses of Parliament when the King was there.

2. They packed a cellar under the Houses of Parliament with barrels of gunpowder, but someone discovered their plot.

3. The plotters were all caught and executed. The most famous of them, Guy Fawkes, was arrested as he guarded the barrels of gunpowder. He is still remembered every year with fireworks and bonfires on the 5th November.

Religion again

James brought in some harsh religious laws: he required people to swear loyalty to him as Head of the Church of England, denying any authority of the Pope. He tried to force the Scottish 'Kirk' to follow the English Church more closely which caused trouble in Scotland as well. But he also had a new English translation of the Bible made. Published in 1611, this 'King James' Bible is considered a masterpiece and is still in use today.

1603	1605	1616
James VI of Scotland becomes James I of the United Kingdom.	The Gunpowder Plot is uncovered. Those involved are executed.	William Shakespeare dies in Stratford-upon-Avon.

During James' reign, the **Mayflower** sailed to America packed with settlers. These people, who became known as the Pilgrim Fathers, formed a colony where they traded with the Native American tribes and planted crops. Many people consider this to be the real start of Europeans colonising North America.

At this time, the Church decided that some women (often healers who used simple herbal remedies) were witches working with the Devil. King James hired witch hunters and thought himself such an expert he even wrote a book on the subject. Thousands of innocent women were terribly treated and many executed during these 'witch hunts'.

You work for the Devil!

We're just trying to heal people.

The divine right of kings

James' son became the next king. Charles I believed even more strongly than his father that he had a 'divine right' to rule. He felt he could make all the decisions about running the country himself without consulting Parliament. When he needed funds for his wars against Spain and France, he raised taxes without permission from his government. The MPs (Members of Parliament) grew angry. They wanted Charles to give them more freedom to run the country, not less – and some were prepared to fight for it!

God has made me king so you must all do exactly what I say!

1620	1625	1629-1640
The *Mayflower* lands at Plymouth Rock, Massachusetts, America.	James I dies and is succeeded by his son, Charles I.	Charles rules without consulting Parliament. MPs grow angry.

The English Civil War

Things came to a head when Charles tried to suspend Parliament and take complete power himself, leading some MPs to call openly for rebellion. Eventually, when Charles tried to arrest some of their leaders, it led to a civil war between the supporters of Parliament and the supporters of King Charles. One strong leader emerged from the Parliamentarians: Oliver Cromwell.

Led by fashionable lords and dukes with long flowing hair, the royalist army of Charles I were called Cavaliers.

The Parliamentarians were known as Roundheads. Their well-disciplined forces became known as the New Model Army. This was the beginning of our modern British army.

You are a traitor to your king, sir!

Surrender!

1642	1644	1645
The English Civil War begins.	Roundheads win the Battle of Marston Moor, west of York.	The Roundheads win the Battle of Naseby, effectively winning the Civil War.

Roundhead victory

Many battles followed with the Scottish army at first supporting the Roundheads. Eventually the Royalists surrendered and King Charles was imprisoned. A Royalist uprising supported by the Scots (who had changed sides) was mercilessly defeated by the New Model Army. Parliament tried to negotiate with Charles in captivity, but later discovered Charles was secretly trying to regain his power with the help of a French invasion. King Charles was tried, found guilty and beheaded as a traitor in 1649.

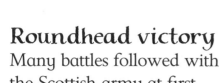

They won't find me up here!

He's here somewhere.

One famous legend tells of Charles' son hiding from the Roundheads in an oak tree before escaping to France. One day he would return to become King Charles II.

'I tell you we will cut off his head with the crown upon it.'

The Commonwealth

This new 'republic' was known as the Commonwealth, with Cromwell as its 'Lord Protector'. His Puritan (a strict sort of Protestant) laws closed down ale houses, theatres and fairs because such pleasures were considered sinful. The Puritans even made Christmas Day a time of fasting not feasting and new churches were built without towers. Cromwell used his army ruthlessly to repress Catholic rebels in both Ireland and Scotland, killing thousands.

1648	1649	1649-1660
Cromwell defeats the Scottish Royalist army and with it a Royalist rebellion.	King Charles I is tried and executed for treason.	The Commonwealth. England and later Scotland and Ireland ruled as a republic.

41

Plague and Fire

After only 11 years, the Commonwealth ended. Cromwell died and, after an unsuccessful attempt by his son to carry on the Puritan regime, Charles II was restored to the throne. This Restoration period saw theatres reopen and Christmas reinstated as a feast day. It saw new fashions and scientific discoveries but also the Great Plague and the Great Fire of London.

The Plague

In 1665 the Great Plague spread through Britain and over a hundred thousand people died in London alone. The sick were confined in their homes, a red cross chalked on the door. Some were treated by special healers; 'plague doctors' wearing strange bird masks filled with sweet smelling herbs. This old rhyme may recall the plague's symptoms:

Ring a ring o' roses,
A pocketful of posies,
Atischo! Atischo! We all fall down.

The Great Fire of London

A year later Thomas Farriner's bakery in Pudding Lane caught fire. The flames quickly spread through the narrow streets lined with ancient wooden houses, but most Londoners escaped with their lives.

1660	1665	1666
Charles II is restored to the throne. Pepys begins his diary.	The Great Plague. It mainly affects London but spreads to other areas of the country.	The Great Fire of London.

We have lost everything.

Samuel Pepys

One famous Londoner, Samuel Pepys, wrote about the Great Fire in his diary. He noted that he buried wine, documents and a valuable Parmesan cheese in his garden to keep them safe from the flames.

Christopher Wren

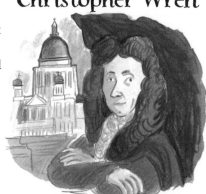

Later, architect Christopher Wren designed large areas of London to be rebuilt in brick and stone. His masterpiece is St Paul's Cathedral.

Sir Isaac Newton

Born in 1643, Newton became one of the most influential scientists ever. His discoveries about the colour spectrum and his designs for telescopes changed the way scientists thought about the world. His famous theory of gravity was supposed to have been inspired by watching an apple fall.

Ah-hah!

Restoration woman

Aphra Behn was the first professional female British writer and she also worked as a spy for Charles II. Under the code-name of Astrea, she spied on English Commonwealth supporters who were plotting against the King.

I was a dramatist, a poet, a writer – and a spy!

1672	**1675**	**1685**
Royal Africa Company set up to control the growing slave trade.	The foundation stone is laid for the new St Paul's Cathedral.	Charles II dies. His brother James II becomes king.

The Glorious Revolution

After Charles II died his brother was crowned King James II. He was openly Roman Catholic and politicians, nobles and the leaders of the Church of England united against him by inviting James' son-in-law, William of Orange, a Dutch Protestant, to land an invasion army and rule instead. James fled the country and William and Mary jointly ruled England, Wales, Scotland and Ireland from 1689 until 1702. Mary's sister Anne then became queen and ruled until 1714.

The first coffee houses opened in Oxford and London in 1652. Men met in them to discuss news, politics and literature. Women were banned!

Rule by Parliament

In 1689, Parliament and William and Mary agreed a Bill of Rights. It ended the worry that a monarch might one day abolish the Church of England or want to rule by 'divine right' as the earlier Stuarts had tried to do.

We rule jointly and have signed a 'contract that future kings and queens must respect the will of Parliament...'

1688-1689
The Glorious Revolution. James II loses the throne to William of Orange and
44   his wife Mary Stuart, both grandchildren of Charles I, in a bloodless rebellion.

1689
William and Mary
sign the Bill of Rights.

The Bank of England moved its headquarters to Threadneedle Street in the heart of the City of London in 1734.

Power and money

When he became king, William was at war with France over his Dutch lands. To raise money for this, he set up the Bank of England in 1694. He also quadrupled the strength of the navy. This boosted both industry and agriculture. The need to build ships and feed sailors began to transform the economy and inspire new ideas about manufacturing and farming as well.

The Jacobites

Because of his support for Roman Catholics and his promise of a free Irish parliament, many Irish and Scottish people were supporters of James Stuart who they still recognised as King James II. They were known as 'Jacobites' and fought for him. But King William's army defeated James' forces at the Battle of the Boyne in Ireland. The defeated Irish were treated very harshly but James was allowed to travel to France in peace. The Jacobites plotted their revenge.

You will be our king...

Our king across the water!

1689
The first Jacobite rebellion in Scotland of supporters of James II.

1690
James II is defeated at the Battle of the Boyne in Ireland. James flees to France.

1702-1714
The reign of Queen Anne, Mary's sister.

45

The Hanoverians

In 1714, the ruler of the small German state of Hanover was crowned George I. He was a great-grandson of James I. Thirteen years later, his son became George II. During this early Georgian period Britain's American colonies grew fast as more people emigrated to make a new life there. British businesses were making fortunes in both the American colonies and also in British-ruled Caribbean islands such as Jamaica and Barbados. Trade was growing not only in cotton, tobacco and sugar but also in African slaves, who were captured and transported across the Atlantic to work on the vast plantations.

In 1768 Captain James Cook set sail on the first of his famous voyages. He mapped and explored regions of the world previously unknown to Europeans, including Australia, New Zealand and many Pacific islands.

The Atlantic slave trade

Sea captains sailed from Britain to Africa, where they traded cloth, rum and other goods for captured West African people. They then took these slaves to North America and the Caribbean to be sold to the owners of sugar and tobacco plantations. The same ships brought back molasses (liquid sugar) or tobacco to Britain. The profits from these goods bought more goods to trade for more slaves. Many people made huge profits from this 'triangular trade'.

It is at this price that Georgians eat sugar and drink rum!

1707	1714	1727
The Act of Union joins the English and Scottish crowns and parliaments, creating Great Britain.	The Hanoverian George I becomes king.	George II becomes king.

Becoming a slave

1. I was captured in West Africa along with my family and sold to British slave dealers. They put me on a ship to Barbados. The journey was dreadful. Many of us died on the way.

2. When we got there, I was sold at auction to a sugar plantation owner. I never saw my family again. As I am young and strong, the traders got a good price for me.

3. Now I work hard planting and cutting sugar cane all day, every day. Our slave drivers whip us if we don't work hard enough.

Why are we fighting with swords and shields against guns and bayonets?

Bonnie Prince Charlie

After years of unsuccessful Jacobite rebellions, Bonnie Prince Charlie, a young Stuart prince, landed in Scotland to lead a new uprising. His Highland army marched as far as Derby gathering English support. However, unable to agree on tactics, they then marched back to Scotland! The brave Highlanders were later massacred by English firepower at the Battle of Culloden. Charlie fled to France never to come back but the rebellious Highland families were punished. Weapons, bagpipes and even kilts were made illegal and many people lost their homes.

My adventures inspired the famous Skye Boat Song: 'Speed bonny boat like a bird on the wing...'

1745	1749	1760
The last Jacobite Rebellion defeated at Culloden in Scotland.	The Bow Street Runners, an early police force, is set up in London.	George III, grandson of George II, becomes king.

Canals, Roads and Martyrs

In the 18th century, the building of canals and road improvements meant coal, cloth and other goods could be transported much more quickly. Better farming techniques meant more food could be produced and the population of Britain doubled from 1737 to 1837. But farm machines replaced men and led to wage cuts. When a group of farm workers from the village of Tolpuddle in Dorset formed a Friendly Society of Agricultural Labourers to support farm worker's rights they were arrested and sentenced to eight years in prison. Known as the Tolpuddle Martyrs, in 1834 they were sent to Botany Bay in Australia, a grim British prison colony. However, protest marches and a petition signed by 800,000 people led to their release.

I'm a bargee on the Leeds-Liverpool canal and I'm taking coal from the Yorkshire mines to Liverpool. Last week I was carrying cloth from the Pennine hills.

Improvements to the roads were funded by tolls collected by Turnpike Trusts. They managed stretches of road and collected money at toll gates.

The Agricultural Revolution

Since feudal times, in some areas farm labourers had shared use of common land to graze their animals and also to grow crops. But a new law, the Enclosure Act of 1773, allowed landowners to turn common land into private estates. Many rural people lost their homes and jobs and moved to the growing towns. Alongside these social changes, farming techniques improved as the estate owners came up with clever ideas.

Bigger and better

Some landowners and farmers, including Robert Bakewell and Thomas Coke, experimented with cross-breeding to produce bigger, healthier animals that gave more milk (cows), wool (sheep) and meat. Coke also realised that some types of grass, such as cocksfoot, made better animal feed.

Mechanical progress

In 1701, Jethro Tull invented a mechanical seed drill which sowed seeds in neat rows. In 1786, Andrew Meikle's threshing machine separated grain from stalk and husk far more quickly and efficiently than before.

Crop rotation

Charles 'Turnip' Townsend and, later, Thomas Coke developed a four-year Norfolk crop rotation. In different fields farmers would plant wheat one year, turnip the next; then barley in year three and clover in year four. Clover actually puts goodness into the soil and along with turnip can be used as animal feed. Then when the field was opened to livestock in those rotation years the animal droppings also added manure to the soil ready for the four-year rotation to begin again.

More Georges

The reign of George III was a time of great change. When Britain's American colonies rebelled against high taxes they were harshly punished. In 1775 the American Revolutionary War began and, under the leadership of George Washington, the independent United States of America came into being. George's reign also saw the French Revolution and the end of the British slave trade. Sadly George III's reign ended in mental illness forcing his son to take over at first as the Prince Regent and then as George IV in 1820.

I am Regent – and a bit of a dandy!

The Boston Tea Party took place in 1773 when American settlers, dressed as Native Americans, protested at high British taxes by throwing valuable chests of tea into Boston harbour.

Hurrah!

William Wilberforce

William Wilberforce was an English politician who headed the parliamentary anti-slavery campaign for 26 years. The Slave Trade Act in 1807 abolished the slave trade in the British Empire and a further act in 1833 ended slavery altogether in British territories.

Architects such as John Nash designed elegant, terraced townhouses in the Regency Style. It was also an age of new styles of fashion for the well-off such as the dandy look of Beau Brummell – which the Prince Regent adopted.

1770s	1773	1783
The Industrial Revolution is underway in Britain.	The first section of the Leeds-Liverpool canal opens.	Britain signs a peace treaty with the now independent United States of America.

During the 18th century, landscape architects such as 'Capability' Brown redesigned the estates of rich landowners; planting trees, digging lakes, and building romantic ruins known as follies. Artists such as Thomas Gainsborough painted the families in their magnificent parklands.

The Napoleonic Wars

In 1789 the French Revolution began. The French executed their king and nobles and formed a republic. Some people worried the same thing would happen in Britain. When the general Napoleon Bonaparte took power in France and began to build a European empire, Britain went to war. In 1805, Admiral Horatio Nelson beat the French and Spanish fleets at the Battle of Trafalgar. Years of war followed until an alliance of countries led by the Duke of Wellington defeated the French army at the Battle of Waterloo in 1815.

The Peterloo Massacre, 1819

Four years later 60,000 people gathered in St Peter's Field in Manchester to protest at new Corn Laws, which were pushing up the cost of bread, and to call for political reform as hardly anyone had the right to vote. Once again, there were fears of revolution. The cavalry were ordered to charge with drawn swords. Eleven people were killed and over 400 injured. Newspapers called it the 'Peterloo Massacre'.

Help!

I was a hero at Waterloo. I am ashamed to say I also fought at Peterloo.

1796	1807	1807	1813	1815
Poet Robert Burns dies.	The slave trade abolished in the British Empire.	Wordsworth writes his 'Daffodils' poem.	Jane Austen's *Pride and Prejudice* is published.	Britain wins the Battle of Waterloo.

Georgian Life

The last Hanoverian king was George IV's brother William. He ended the Georgian era, an era that had seen giant leaps forward in industry, farming and science. This was also the age of romantic poetry, literature and art.

I love poetry and I find my fashion tips in The Lady magazine.

Fashion

Corsets, tightly laced underwear, had been used to shape a woman's figure for hundreds of years, but in the 1700s whalebone stays made corsets even tighter, restricting breathing and squeezing internal organs.

Dances, often held in local assembly rooms, were a way for wealthy young Georgians to meet suitable matches.

Robert Burns

'My love is like a red red rose That 's newly sprung in June.'

'I wandered lonely as a cloud That floats on high o'er vales and hills, When all at once I saw a crowd, A host, of golden daffodils...'

William Wordsworth

Poetry and novels

Georgians loved to read poets such as: Lord Byron, William Wordsworth, Robert Burns, John Keats, William Blake and Samuel Coleridge. Georgians also loved novels such as: Jonathan Swift's *Gulliver's Travels*, Daniel Defoe's *Robinson Crusoe*, Mary Shelley's *Frankenstein* and Jane Austen's *Pride and Prejudice*.

1818	1820	1821
Mary Shelley's *Frankenstein* is published.	The Regency ends when George IV becomes king.	Michael Faraday discovers electro-magnetic rotations.

Artists

Romantic artists of the age included the artists J M W Turner, John Constable and Thomas Gainsborough as well as 'visionary' painters such as William Blake and John Martin. There were also enamel miniature painters such as Charles Muss and political illustrators such as William Hogarth (in the early half of the 1700s) and later George Cruikshank and James Gillray.

Jane Austen's novels were romances that questioned the manners and behaviour of wealthy families.

The painter J M W Turner once tied himself to a ship's mast to paint a stormy seascape.

Scientist Michael Faraday investigated electro-magnetism. This led to the technology of electric motors and the eventual practical use of electricity.

Mary Shelley's **Frankenstein** was a horror story. Hearing about the latest scientific research inspired her to bring Frankenstein's monster to life using electricity.

Crime and punishment

Another author, Henry Fielding, was also one of the founders of the first organised police force – the Bow Street Runners founded in 1749. Later in 1829 came Robert Peel's police force known as 'Peelers'.

Stand and deliver – your money or your life!

Many crimes, even petty shoplifting and pickpocketing, carried the death penalty. Crowds of people would gather to watch a public hanging, often buying 'broadsheets', cheaply printed leaflets about the criminals' deeds. Criminals such as the highwayman Dick Turpin became romantic folk heroes.

1825
The first passenger railway, from Stockton to Darlington, opens.

1830
George IV dies and his brother William IV becomes king.

1834
The Tolpuddle Martyrs are transported to Australia.

53

Industrial Revolution

Hand-loom workers had been weaving cloth in a home-based, cottage industry since the 14th century. But in the 1700s new mechanical inventions took over – flying shuttles, spinning jennies and powered looms began mass-producing textiles in newly built mills. These mills relied on waterpower at first, but by the 1770s James Watt's steam engines were powering all sorts of factory machines. Towns mushroomed as people flocked to work in the mills and factories. Along with Abraham Darby's use of coke (a fuel made from coal) to smelt iron, the invention of early coal-hauling steam locomotives and new developments in firing pottery, Britain began to revolutionise world industry.

The noise makes my ears hurt and the air is full of cotton fluff. I cough all the time.

The first locomotives were invented to haul coal wagons along metal tracks in factory yards. But in 1829, *Rocket*, a new design by Robert and George Stephenson, won a competition held by the Liverpool and Manchester Railway for the world's first true passenger-hauling locomotives. The railway opened for business in 1830.

I'm a scavenger – I clean the fluff from under the machinery. My friend lost a finger last week. He is only nine years old.

This mill is in Bradford and we are weaving cotton textiles.

Other mills weave wool to make worsted, flax to make linen and even silk.

A mill girl

Smash it up!

1. My dad was a home-weaver until he lost his job. He blamed the machines and joined a gang called Luddites who smashed them up. But he was arrested and sent to Botany Bay in Australia.

2. My brother is eight and he works down a coal mine pushing coal trucks all day. My mum and I work here in this mill. It's long hours but it puts food on the table!

I am 12 and I work long hours but I operate dangerous weaving machines so I must not get tired.

The Victorians

In 1837 Queen Victoria, a granddaughter of George III, became queen. Her reign would last over 63 years and would see long periods of peace and prosperity. The Industrial Revolution went from strength to strength, producing many amazing inventions. British power grew overseas, too, despite later wars in the Crimea and South Africa. At home, social campaigners highlighted the hardship of the poor. Slowly things began to change.

Electoral reform

Britain had long been divided into 'seats' which elected politicians to represent their region as members of parliament (MPs). The party with the most seats formed the government. However, many of the growing towns were not represented at all, while small rural areas such as Old Sarum, with only seven people who could vote, had two MPs! The first Reform Act of 1832 had begun to change this. It also gave more men voting rights, if they lived in a town or owned property. More reforms followed in the Victorian era, as the House of Commons became more truly representative of British men – but no women could vote.

Queen Victoria married her German cousin, Prince Albert of Saxe-Coburg. He introduced the fashion for Christmas trees from his homeland in 1840.

Merry Christmas!

The Christmas tree became very popular, especially with the new middle class created by the Industrial Revolution: office workers, shopkeepers, bank and train clerks...

Two political parties fought for power at the time: the Conservatives (known as Tories) and the Liberals (known as Whigs). The best-known Tory Prime Minister was Benjamin Disraeli; whilst William Gladstone was the Liberal's most famous Prime Minister.

I'm Disraeli.

I'm Gladstone.

1833	1837	1838	1841
The first Factory Act is passed to improve working conditions.	Victoria becomes queen.	Charles Dickens' *Oliver Twist* is published.	Fox Talbot patents his photographic process.

Dickens' child characters

Tiny Tim: a poor, disabled boy who gets his Christmas dinner!

More?

Oliver Twist: a workhouse child forced to become a pickpocket.

David Copperfield: a boy made to work in a factory, like Dickens himself.

Little Nell: an orphan girl chased by wicked adults.

As a 12-year-old, when his father was sent to prison for owing money, Charles Dickens had been forced to work in a boot polish factory. Later, he wrote books such as **David Copperfield** and **Oliver Twist** about the exploitation of children and the terrible conditions they faced.

Emily Brontë wrote about a starving Liverpool urchin, named Heathcliff, brought to live on the Yorkshire moors. Published in 1847, her romantic novel **Wuthering Heights** about Heathcliff and Cathy still thrills readers today.

Child labour

As the towns grew, so did the crowded slums. Families had to send their children out to work to pay for food and rent. Boys and girls as young as six had to work up to 16 hours a day, six days a week in mills, factories and mines; or as chimney sweeps and match sellers. Slowly, campaigners such as Lord Shaftesbury brought about change. Various factory acts improved the working conditions of children by law, reducing hours, enforcing safety and making employers provide some schooling.

My books about the poor inspired public sympathy and brought about change.

I'm forced to climb up inside chimneys to sweep them.

1843	1844	1845
Brunel's steamship SS *Great Britain* launched.	5,000 miles of railway track are laid across Britain. JMW Turner exhibits his painting *Rain, Steam and Speed*.	The start of the Irish Potato Famine.

Britain Can Make It!

The Victorian era saw many important inventions. The development of powerful steam locomotives and railway networks, steam ships, early photography and the first electric light bulbs were just some of the things Britain could be proud of. The Great Exhibition of 1851 was held in the specially built Crystal Palace to show off British skills and expertise to the world. Sadly in 1861 Prince Albert died. Queen Victoria was heart-broken. She wore black for the rest of her life.

Hello?

Alexander Graham Bell designed and patented a telephone in 1876.

Queen Victoria reigned for 63 years.

I K Brunel developed the Great Western Railway network and then extended train travel to America – by building 'trains of the sea': steam-powered, iron-hulled ships such as the SS **Great Britain**.

Albert advised me to keep out of politics. I prefer to spend my time at Balmoral in Scotland now.

In 1841, photographic pioneer William Fox Talbot invented a way to make multiple copies of one photograph from a single negative image.

Smile!

1851	1853-1856	1859
The Great Exhibition, promoted by Prince Albert, held in London.	The Crimean War is fought in the Crimean Peninsula on the Black Sea.	Darwin publishes his masterwork *On the Origin of Species.*

The Irish Potato Famine

The Irish Potato Famine was a period of mass starvation between 1845 and 1852. It was caused by massive crop failures due to a potato disease called potato blight. Approximately a million people died while another million emigrated to places such as America and Australia. It brought great resentment of English landlords and British rule and rallied republicans and their calls for independence from Britain.

> They call me the lady with the lamp.

The Crimean War

In 1854, Britain found itself at war again – this time against Russia in the Crimean Peninsula. Newspaper reports home told of the terrible conditions in the hospitals and how many wounded soldiers were dying unnecessarily. Florence Nightingale, famous already for her nursing reforms, was asked to help out. A Jamaican-born nurse called Mary Seacole also became famous for helping troops in the Crimea.

> My book shook the world!

Charles Darwin

In 1859, Darwin published *On The Origin of Species*, a book that put forward his theory of evolution by natural selection. He showed how animals that adapted to their environment did best, even changing (evolving) new body shapes and feeding habits over generations as their skills and strengths were passed on. Because his theory contradicted the Bible by suggesting that humans had evolved from apes and not from Adam and Eve it caused outrage with many religious leaders.

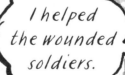

> I helped the wounded soldiers.

1870	1871	1876
The Education Act sets up more primary schools.	The Trade Union Act makes trade unions legal.	Disraeli, the Prime Minister, makes Queen Victoria Empress of India.

Victoria's Empire

For hundreds of years the British Empire had been growing as Britain laid claim to more regions of the world, boosting its profits in timber, precious metals, spices, tea, tobacco, furs, wool, cotton, salt, gold, diamonds and many other things. The lands of the British Empire under Queen Victoria's rule are coloured in red on this blackboard. They were controlled by strong British administrators and protected by British military power on land and sea. In 1876, at the suggestion of Disraeli, Victoria was proclaimed Empress of India.

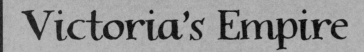

Britain and India

The East India Company was set up in 1600 to trade with India and the Far East. In India, its power became so great that by the mid-18th century is was effectively running the country. In 1858, the British government took over direct rule of India, making India part of its empire. The British Raj ('Raj' means 'rule' in Hindi) not only brought huge wealth to Britain but also new words such as jungle, pyjamas and chutney. Indians fought bravely for Britain in many wars.

School for all

Until 1870 all schools were private or run by charities. The 1870 Education Act created primary schools paid for by local taxes. A further act in 1880 made it compulsory for 5-to-13-year-olds to attend. Some people actually opposed education for all, worried that educating the working classes might lead to revolution! Later laws allowed local authorities to create secondary schools and abolished fees for primary schools.

The Edwardians

After Queen Victoria's death in 1901, her son became King Edward VII. Life was changing fast and the start of a new century would see amazing inventions we take for granted today: motor cars, cinemas, flying machines, not to mention changes in fashion styles, jazz music and new art. However, many children still suffered from stunted growth due to lack of food. New laws, including the provision of free school meals, formed the beginning of what would later become the Welfare State. The Edwardian era also saw the rise of the trade union movement but also the international rivalry that would lead to the First World War.

In 1909, John Moore-Brabazon, an aviator and politician, was the first Englishman to fly an aeroplane in Britain.

I am King Edward but everyone calls me Bertie!

The motor car

Like many wealthy people by this time, King Edward owned a motor car (first invented in the 1880s). Edward's car was a German-built Daimler but in 1906 Herbert Austin's new production line factory in Worcestershire was building Austins. They would become one of the most well-known British cars. In 1913, the American car manufacturer Henry Ford opened a factory in Manchester and his famous Model T Ford went into production in the UK.

1899-1902
The Second Boer War is fought in South Africa.

1901
Edward VII becomes king.

1906
Local councils start to give free school meals to poor families.

Come on, chaps!

British Antarctic explorers like Ernest Shackleton and Robert Scott became famous. Scott's race to the South Pole in 1912 made him a hero, even though Scott lost the race and died on the way back.

'Iceberg, dead ahead!'

The ultra-modern **Titanic** passenger ship claimed to be unsinkable. But, in 1912, when it hit an iceberg while steaming to America, it sank quickly, and because there were not enough lifeboats around 15,000 people lost their lives, mostly the poorer passengers.

We demand the vote for women!

Suffragettes

In the early 20th century, women were becoming more independent and some were going to university and becoming doctors, but they still could not vote. In 1903, led by Emmeline Pankhurst, the suffragettes began to campaign for women's right to vote. Suffragettes were often put in prison and roughly treated but they didn't give up.

VOTES

1910
Edward VII dies. His son becomes George V.

1909
Imprisoned suffragette, Marion Wallace Dunlop, goes on hunger strike.

1912
Scott dies in Antarctica; the same year the *Titanic* sinks.

The First World War

In 1914, Franz Ferdinand, the heir to the throne of Austria-Hungary, was assassinated by a Bosnian Serb called Gavrilo Princip. Austria-Hungary declared war on Serbia with German support and this acted as a trigger for something far bigger as country after country was pulled into war by their alliances. When Germany invaded Belgium on its way to attack France, Britain got involved as it had promised to protect Belgium. The First World War had begun. At first young men on both sides rushed to join up thinking it was going to be a comic book adventure, the 'derring-do' of the *Boys Own* paper. But they soon discovered war isn't really like comic books at all.

1 July 1916, the first day of the Battle of the Somme, was the worst day in the history of the British army. About 40,000 men were injured and 20,000 killed by machine guns and artillery fire.

The constant explosions were too much for some lads. You'd call it shell shock, but some of our officers called it cowardice. You could be executed by firing squad for that!

I don't want to go over the top, Sarge.

1914	July-November 1916	September 1916
The First Word War begins.	The Battle of the Somme. Over 1,000,000 men, from all sides, are wounded or killed.	Britain uses tanks for the first time in battle.

Women played their part, too, working on farms and in the ammunition factories. Many earned the nickname 'canary girls' because their skin turned yellow due to exposure to explosive chemicals. Some even died from the poisonous fumes and accidents.

Poets such as Wilfred Owen wrote about the reality of trench warfare. The composer Ralph Vaughan Williams composed his famous **Pastoral Symphony** in 1921, lamenting the millions killed.

'Men marched asleep.
Many had lost their boots
But limped on, blood-shod...'

A new kind of war

The war was fought on many 'fronts' from Northern Europe to Palestine and the Middle East, involving soldiers from many countries. The Allies included Britain, Canada, Australia, New Zealand, India and France; they fought against Germany, Austria-Hungary, Turkey and some others. This was a new kind of warfare: new weapons, such as high-explosive shells and the Vickers machine gun that fired 500 bullets a minute, revolutionised killing. Evenly matched, neither army could push forward for victory so they dug trenches across the countryside.

Artillery (big guns) fired barrages of high-explosive shells at each other, destroying villages, fields and trees and leaving a landscape of shell craters and mud. Soldiers were ordered 'over the top' to try and capture only a few hundred metres of enemy held ground. As the war claimed more lives ordinary people were called up by law to fight. The war lasted until November 1918 when Germany finally surrendered, leaving a world total of about 16 million dead and 20 million wounded.

1917
The USA join the war on the side of Britain and its allies.

4 November 1918
Poet Wilfred Owen is killed in action.

11 November 1918
Fighting stops. Germany is defeated and a peace treaty is signed.

Between the Wars

After Germany and her allies surrendered in 1918, British soldiers came home to a hero's welcome. Many were shocked and sickened by what they had done and seen on the battlefields. Parts of Britain's empire, such as Canada, Australia and India, had a surge of national pride that pushed their leaders to ask for more independence from Britain. From the 1920s into the 1930s, economic depression led to massive unemployment, with strikes for wage rises and protest marches. In 1933, the racist Nazi Party, led by the dictator Adolf Hitler, had taken over Germany. He wanted revenge for Germany's defeat in 1918. By the late 1930s, war seemed likely again.

At last, women can vote.

Soon after the war, men over 21 and married women over 30 were given the vote. Women's active part in the war helped their cause. But it wasn't until 1928 that all men and women aged 21 or over were given the right to vote.

We are flappers!

We love to dance!

By the 1920s dance crazes like the Charleston and short 'flapper' dresses shocked older people who had grown up as Victorians. The first cinemas showed silent moving films, featuring stars such as Charlie Chaplin. By the 1930s, there were 'talking' pictures.

1922	1924	1928
Independent Irish Free State formed.	First ever Labour government, led by Ramsay MacDonald.	All men and women aged 21 and over gain the right to vote.

The Irish Free State

Between 1919 and 1921, the Irish Republican Army (IRA) fought for Irish independence against British government forces and Irish Loyalist supporters. In 1922, Ireland became the Irish Free State but six counties in the north opted out of the agreement to rejoin the United Kingdom as Northern Ireland. This led to unrest and terrorist bomb attacks against civilians took place in both Ireland and the mainland UK. Such violence would last for decades until the 1998 Good Friday Agreement brought peace.

Freedom for Ireland!

A new decorative art style known as Art Deco took the world by storm in the 1920s and 30s. The sleek, geometric shapes could be seen in everything from buildings to cars and in everyday objects such as radios and the cup and saucer designs of Susie Cooper. British modernist painters of the time included Paul Nash, Winifred Nicholson and Eric Ravilious.

The trade unions

Through the 1900s, the trade union movement (organisations of working people) grew steadily using their unity to negotiate better conditions and pay. It didn't always work; in 1926 the General Strike failed and one million miners were forced to accept wage cuts. The unions supported a new political party founded in 1900: the Labour Party, a socialist party, who put the workers first. By the 1920s they had overtaken the Liberal Party in many elections. The first Labour governments took place in 1924 and 1929-31.

In 1936, I marched 300 miles from Jarrow to London as one of 200 protestors. We wanted people to know about our unemployment – and our hunger.

1929
Susie Cooper opens her own pottery.

October 1936
Workers from Jarrow, near Newcastle-upon-Tyne, march to London.

December 1936
Edward VIII, king for less than a year, abdicates. His brother George VI is now king. 67

The Second World War

Adolf Hitler's German army invaded Poland in 1939, forcing Britain to declare war in support of their Polish allies. An Expeditionary Force of British troops was sent to Europe, but was quickly defeated. In May 1940, many managed to retreat home to Britain from Dunkirk but lost much of their equipment and weapons. Things looked bleak when the Nazis captured the Channel Islands and began to drop bombs on Britain in preparation for an invasion. But the Royal Air Force fought back and during the Battle of Britain the RAF shot down so many Luftwaffe aircraft that the Germans gave up their plans to invade Britain.

I miss my mum.

Children were evacuated from heavily bombed cities and sent for safety to the countryside. Many were unhappy and missed their homes.

Up you come, lad!

I am Winston Churchill, the war-time British Prime Minister famous for my stirring speeches. 'We will never surrender!'

In May 1940, the British and French army was trapped on the beaches of Dunkirk in France. Helped by many small civilian boats, the Royal Navy made a daring rescue transporting almost 350,000 soldiers back to Britain.

1939
Start of the Second World War.

1940
British forces retreat from Dunkirk. The German airforce bombs British cities.

1941
RAF fights back with bombing campaigns on Germany.

Britain relied on extra food and military supplies brought from the USA by the merchant navy, but Nazi submarines torpedoed their ships and many sailors were killed.

Women at war

Many women joined the forces such as the WAAF (the Women's Auxiliary Air Force) and the WRENS (Women's Royal Naval Service). Others worked in factories or as landgirls. Some brave women were sent to France as spies to help the French Resistance. Many, such as Noor Inayat Khan, were caught and executed by the Nazis.

At first Britain could only fight back with its airforce. RAF bomber squadrons flew night raids across the sea to attack Nazi targets. Many RAF bomber crews were killed; a tail-gunner for example was lucky to survive more than three missions.

RAF fighter and bomber crews fought bravely.

War against Japan

In 1941, Germany's ally Japan invaded the British Empire in Asia, taking territory and cruelly treating thousands of captured British and Commonwealth prisoners. But the Japanese also attacked the USA's naval base at Pearl Harbor in Hawaii and this brought the USA into the war to fight alongside Britain and her allies. Slowly the tide began to turn. On D-Day, 1944, Allied forces landed in France and despite great loss of life, fought their way inland.

In May 1945, 'Victory in Europe' was celebrated in street parties across Britain. Yet the war against Japan continued. Finally the devastating use of the newly invented atom bomb on two cities, Nagasaki and Hiroshima, forced Japan's surrender in September 1945.

1943	1944	1945
Bletchley code-breakers are cracking coded German messages.	After D-Day, Allied troops fight their way into Europe.	War ends. Germany surrenders in May; Japan in September.

The Age of Austerity

By 1946, years of war had left Britain almost bankrupt, forcing the country to borrow money from the USA and Canada (loans that wouldn't be paid off until 2006). This time was known as the 'age of austerity', as wartime rationing continued and Britain slowly rebuilt itself.

My name is Bond, James Bond.

Fear of nuclear war created the Campaign for Nuclear Disarmament known as CND. The Cold War also inspired the fictional spy James Bond, created by Ian Fleming.

It's jelly for pudding.

Before the National Health Service you had to pay to see a doctor.

Time for change

During the war, the political parties had shared power led by the Conservative Winston Churchill. But in 1945 the Labour Party came to power in a landslide victory. The new prime minister, Clement Atlee, created a stronger system of support for poorer people: the Welfare State. It included the National Health Service that gave people free medical care. The government also took control of many key industries such as the railways, coal and steel.

The Cold War

By 1946, the wartime alliance between Britain and the USA with the Soviet Union had broken down. The Cold War was an uneasy time when the risk of a devastating nuclear war between the Western powers and the Communist powers dominated by the Soviet Union seemed very real.

1947	1948	1951
Railways nationalised (brought under government control).	492 Jamaican immigrants arrive in Britain aboard *Empire Windrush*.	Festival of Britain showcases British skills, boosting post-war morale.

Rock'n'roll

Slowly things 'came off the ration' and all rationing finally ended in 1954. The 1950s saw a upturn in the economy and by the late 50s something completely new arrived from America and took root; music and fashion for teenagers. Jazz and rock'n'roll music played in clubs and coffee bars became cool. British rockers such as Tommy Steele and Marty Wilde led the BBC to make the first youth TV show *The Six-Five Special* in 1957. An explosion of youth culture was on its way.

Let's rock 'n'roll.

In 1948, *Empire Windrush* brought the first post-war immigrants from Jamaica in the British West Indies. Immigrants also arrived from Poland and the Ukraine as well as Asian people from Hong Kong, Malaysia and India and Pakistan (India had gained independence in 1947, splitting into two states). As immigrants had done before, these new arrivals enriched British life and introduced new music, fashion and foods.

In 1952, George VI who had been king during World War Two died and his daughter Elizabeth became queen. Her coronation in 1953 boosted people's spirits in post-war Britain.

My coronation is the start of a new Elizabethan age.

1952
Elizabeth II becomes queen. Her coronation in 1953 is televised.

1955
US hit 'Rock around the Clock' is the UK number 1 single.

1958
First CND march on Aldermaston, where nuclear weapons are held.

The Fab 1960s

By the early 1960s Britain's youth had begun to develop a new style of music. 'Beat' music was pop-rock with a toe-tapping beat led by new bands such as The Beatles, from Liverpool. They took the world by storm. As teenagers spent their wages, music and fashion evolved quickly alongside trends in the world of literature, art and design. Artists such as Eduardo Paolozzi and Bridget Riley, poets including Ted Hughes and Roger McGough and designers such as Mary Quant were all part of a huge revival in British self-confidence. Harold Wilson's Labour Party governed a country on the rise. But trade union strikes and troubles in Northern Ireland loomed.

In 1966 millions tuned in to watch the England football team win the World Cup.

The Beatles caused a fan hysteria known as 'Beatlemania' wherever they went. They opened the door for other British pop acts: The Rolling Stones, The Kinks, The Moody Blues, Sandy Shaw and The Animals to name just a few.

YEAH!

YEAH!

YEAH!

Let's watch TV

By the 1960s most people owned a television and it was the main source of news and entertainment. The first episode of the children's time-travel adventure series *Doctor Who* was broadcast in 1963 and in 1964 came the first episode of the pop music show *Top of the Pops*. 1969 was the year everyone saw the American astronaut Neil Armstrong walk on the Moon live on TV. In the late 1960s and early 70s, many families switched from black-and-white to colour TVs as they slowly became more affordable.

1963
The Beatles have three number 1 hits in the UK.

1964
Labour government elected. Harold Wilson is Prime Minister.

1965
Comprehensive schools open in many parts of the UK.

From 1944, children had taken a test at 11 to see what sort of secondary school they went to – a grammar school for those who passed or a secondary modern for the rest. This was thought by many to be unfair and so in the mid-1960s comprehensive schools were introduced where children of all abilities and both sexes studied together.

Terence Conran's new store, Habitat, opened in 1964. Its bright colours, pine and inexpensive wipe-clean modern plastics revolutionised styles in the home. In the same year Polish-born Barbara Hulanicki opened her shop Biba in London, selling up-to-date, affordable fashions to the growing number of independent, free-thinking women.

Welcome to the fab 60s!

1966
England beats West Germany to win the football World Cup.

1967
Roger McGough's poetry anthology *The Mersey Sound* is published.

1969
TV comedy show *Monty Python's Flying Circus* goes on air.

Hippy to Punk 70s~80s

By the 1970s music and fashion had developed into many styles: hippy, skinhead, rocker, reggae and soul all had their own 'look'. 'Glam rock' artists such as David Bowie and Marc Bolan wore crazy make-up and their screaming young fans inspired a new word: teenyboppers. By the early 1980s digital CDs were replacing scratchy records and hissing cassette tapes as the best way to play music. Meanwhile green issues were catching the public interest.

Reggae music came to Britain with immigrants from Jamaica.

Hippies promoted peace and a love of nature and ancient mysteries such as Stonehenge. Outdoor rock festivals at such ancient 'magical' sites became popular, attended by thousands of young people.

LOVE NOT WAR

Peace, Man!

1970	1973	1974
Over 600,000 people attend the Isle of Wight rock festival.	Britain joins the European Economic Community (EEC).	21 killed when the IRA bomb a pub in Birmingham.

The 1970s saw some of the worst troubles in Northern Ireland between the IRA and Loyalist groups backed by the British Army. Terrorists from both sides attacked civilians and soldiers. In 1972 British soldiers opened fire on Republican protesters and bystanders killing 14 people. The violence continued until peace was made and the IRA announced an end to its armed campaign in 2005.

The Women's Liberation Movement formed to fight for equal rights and opportunities for women. The first women's lib march took place in London in 1971.

God save the Queen!

Punk

From about 1977 the exciting sound of punk rock dominated British music and fashion. Bands such as The Clash, The Sex Pistols and X-Ray Spex took Britain by storm. Punk was followed by other new styles, some using electronic sounds or computer-driven technology while others sampled punk and hippy styles to create house and rave music. US street music such as hip-hop also caught on in the UK.

1977
Queen Elizabeth's Silver Jubilee. Many street parties are held.

1978-79
Many trade unions strike during 'the Winter of Discontent'.

1979
Margaret Thatcher becomes Britain's first female prime minister.

Into the 21st Century

In the 1980s one of the biggest revolutions of all took place as computers began to appear in homes and offices. By the 1990s the development of 3D computer games, mobile phones and the Internet changed our world. Britain had been a member of the European Economic Community since 1973. In 1993 this became the European Union, sharing trade, some political decisions and the right to work within other member states. In 1998 Scotland and Wales were given limited rights to make their own laws. The story of Britain continues . . .

Everyone mourned the death of Diana, Princess of Wales, killed in a car crash in 1997. In 2011, the nation celebrated the marriage of her son Prince William to Kate and the birth of their baby George in 2013.

Governments and unions

In 1979, Margaret Thatcher, a Conservative, became Britain's first woman prime minister. In 1984, her planned closure of 70 coal mines caused strikes but, despite violent battles fought between police and miners, the pit closures went ahead. There was lot of bitterness as close-knit mining communities splintered, while the power of the trade unions was never as strong after this. In 1997 Labour won power under Tony Blair.

Vote New Labour!

People called me the 'Iron Lady'. I was a popular prime minister with some people, but unpopular with many others. . .

1982	1984-1985	1985
Britain wins the Falkland War against Argentina.	The Miners' Strike fails to stop the government's proposed pit closures.	The Live Aid concert raises millions for African famine victims.

Britain still fought in wars; in 1982 Margaret Thatcher went to war with Argentina to protect the residents of a small left-over of the British Empire, the Falkland Islands. Britain also supported the USA during the Gulf War (1990-91). Later, in response to terrorist attacks on America and Britain, Tony Blair took the UK to war in Afghanistan in 2001 and Iraq in 2003.

Conservation, protection of wildlife and green issues become even more important. As people began to feel the effects of global warming, recycling bins were introduced in many areas.

Thousands of years have gone by – and now you are part of the story of Britain!

Computers and 'the web'

Computer technology, developed by Alan Turing and Tommy Flowers during the Second World War to crack German secret codes, spread across the world eventually giving us the home computers we all use today. In 1989, Tim Berners-Lee invented the World Wide Web and revolutionised the way we think, learn, play and talk to each other!

THE STORY OF BRITAIN
Mick Manning & Brita Granström

1989	1997	1998
Tim Berners-Lee invents the World Wide Web.	After 18 years of Conservative rule, Labour wins power.	Scottish and Welsh assemblies formed with limited power to make their own laws.

From way back when ...

The world has never been the same since the Brits got thinking and creating. Here are just a few more great things about Great Britain. We couldn't fit anything else in but there are loads more . . . What would you choose?

William Blake, poet and painter

Robert FitzRoy's Met Office

Cricketers such as W G Grace

The first chocolate bars by Fry's

Bowler Hats

Edward Lear's limericks

Hubert Cecil Booth's electric vacuum cleaner

Joseph Swan's lightbulb

The first TV invented by John Logie Baird

... and a British Cuppa!

Fish and chips, first brought to Britain by Jewish refugees and now a national dish

The first jet engine invented by Frank Whittle

Robert Watson-Watt's British radar

78

Poets old and new, including Dylan Thomas and Benjamin Zephaniah

Children's authors including Roald Dahl and J K Rowling

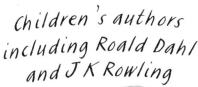

Punk heroes such as Poly Styrene and Johnny Rotten

TV shows such as **Monty Python** and **Dr Who**

Spicy curries and Asian restaurants

Scientists such as Stephen Hawking

British classical music such as Vaughan Williams' **Lark Ascending**

Modern British artists such as Henry Moore and David Hockney

... to here right now

But history isn't just about 'famous' people, it's about you and me; it's about our mums and dads and their mums and dads. Our ancestors settled here or were born here and they have lived through the history in this book from way back then to here right now. Their history is your history too; in fact history leads right up to the very moment that you read these words . . . and beyond. So, what's next?

British sporting heroes such as David Beckham

World music stars such as Sheila Chandra

Index

Act of Union 46
Afghanistan 77
Agricultural Revolution 48-49
America 39, 46, 50
Anglo-Saxons 14-17, 21, 23
artists 51-53, 57, 67, 72, 79
Australia 46, 48, 53, 55, 59, 61, 65, 66
Battle of Agincourt 28
Battle of Bannockburn 27
Battle of Bosworth 29
Battle of the Boyne 45
Battle of Culloden 47
Battle of Hastings 18, 19
Battle of Waterloo 51
Beaker People 5
Becket, Bishop Thomas 22, 24
Bede 14-15
Beowulf 15
Bill of Rights 44
Black Death 28, 31
Bonnie Prince Charlie 47
British Empire 50-51, 59-61, 66, 77
Bronze Age 4-5
Brunel, Isambard Kingdom 57-58
Caesar, Julius 10
Campaign for Nuclear Disarmament (CND) 70-71
canals 48-50
cars 62
Caxton, William 29, 31
Celts 8-9, 10, 14
Chaucer, Geoffrey 29, 31
Church of England 32-33, 38, 44
Churchill, Winston 68, 70
Cold War 70
computers 76-77
Cook, Captain James 46
Crimean War 56, 58-59
Cromwell, Oliver 40-42
Cromwell, Thomas 33
Crusades 24, 26
Danelaw, the 16-17
Darwin, Charles 58-59
Dickens, Charles 56-57
Doggerland 2-3

Domesday Book 19
Drake, Sir Francis 34-35
education 59-63, 72-73
Edwardians 62-63
elections 56, 67
Enclosure Act 49
engines, steam 54
English Civil War 40-41
European Economic Community/ European Union 74, 76
explorers 34-35, 46, 63
factory life 54-55, 57
Falklands War 76, 77
farming 4-5, 14, 17, 20-21, 31, 45, 48-49, 52, 65
fashion 42, 50, 52, 62, 66, 71, 72-73, 74-75
feudalism 20-21, 49
First World War 62, 64-66
France 8, 18-19, 22, 24, 25, 27, 28, 35, 39, 41, 45, 47, 50, 51, 64-65, 68, 69
French Revolution 50-51
Georgians 46-56
Glorious Revolution 44-45
Great Exhibition 58
Great Fire of London 42-43
Great Plague 42
Gruffydd, Llywelyn ap 26
guilds 30
Gulf War 77
Gunpowder Plot 38
Hadrian's Wall 10-11
Hitler, Adolf 66, 68
Hundred Years' War 28-29
Ice Age 2-3
immigration 70-71, 74
India 35, 59, 60-61, 65, 71
Industrial Revolution 48-51, 54-56
industry, wool 31, 54
inventors 54, 56-58, 62, 77-79
Iraq War 77
Ireland 15, 16, 17, 23, 38, 41, 44, 45, 57, 59, 66-67
Irish Free State 66, 67
Irish Potato Famine 57, 59

Iron Age 8-9
Jacobites 45, 47
Jamaica 46, 60, 71, 74
Jarrow March 67
King Alfred 17
King Canute 17
King Charles I 39-41, 44
King Charles II 41-43
King Edward I (Longshanks) 26-27
King Edward VI 32-33
King Henry II 22-24
King Henry V 28
King Henry VIII 30, 32-33
King James I 35, 38-39, 46
King John 25-26
King Richard I (the Lionheart) 23-25
King Richard III 29
King William I (the Conqueror) 18-19, 22
King William and Queen Mary 44-45
Lindisfarne 15-16
Magna Carta 25
Mary, Queen of Scots 35, 38
Miners' Strike 76
monasteries 15-16, 33
music 36, 62, 65, 71-72, 74-75, 79
Napoleonic Wars 51
National Health Service 70
Newton, Sir Isaac 43
Normans 18-22
Northern Ireland 67, 72, 74, 75
nuclear war 70
Peasants' Revolt 29, 31
Pepys, Samuel 42-43
Peterloo Massacre 51
Plantagenets 22-29
plays, mystery 30, 37
Princess Diana 76
Queen Elizabeth I 32, 34-38
Queen Elizabeth II 71-77
Queen Victoria 56-62
railways 53-54, 57, 58, 70
Reformation 32-33

religion 4, 7, 10, 13, 15, 17, 22, 24, 32-36, 38-39, 41, 42, 44
Robert the Bruce 27
Romans 9-14
scientists 43, 52, 53, 79
Scotland 9, 10-11, 15, 16, 17, 19, 22, 26-27, 32, 35, 38-39, 41, 44-45, 46, 47, 76-77
Scott, Robert 63
Second World War 68-69, 77
Shakespeare, William 34-38
South Africa 56, 60-61, 62
Spanish Armada 35
Stone Age 2-5
Stonehenge 4-8, 74
Strongbow (Richard de Clare) 23
suffragettes 63
television 71, 72, 73, 78-79
Thatcher, Margaret 75, 76, 77
Titanic 63
Tolpuddle Martyrs 48-49, 53
tools 2, 5, 7, 8
trade 17, 30-31, 46-48, 60-61, 76
trade, slave 43, 46-47, 50, 51
trade unions 59, 62, 67, 72, 75, 76
Tudors 29-38
USA 50, 58, 59, 62-63, 65, 69, 70, 71, 72, 75, 77
Victorians 56-62
Vikings 15-18
vote, the 51, 56, 63, 66, 67
Wales 14, 19, 26, 27, 35, 38, 41, 76-77
Wallace, William 27
Wars of the Roses 29
weapons 5, 7-8, 10-11, 18, 28, 47, 65, 68-71
weaving 5, 9, 31, 54-55
Welfare State 62, 70
Women's Liberation Movement 75
working conditions 54-57
writers 29, 31, 34-38, 43, 51-53, 56, 57, 65, 72, 73, 78-79

To Rachel Cooke with love from Mick and Brita

Franklin Watts
Published in Great Britain in 2016 by The Watts Publishing Group

Text and illustrations © Mick Manning and Brita Granström 2015

Mick and Brita made the illustrations for this book. Find out more at www.mickandbrita.com.
Editor: Rachel Cooke; Additional editorial work and consultancy: Sarah Ridley; Design: Jonathan Hair and Sophie Pelham based on original layouts by Mick and Brita.

You can visit many of the places mentioned in this book and find many of the treasures it names in museums around the country.

Dewey Classification: 941
ISBN: 978 1 4451 2788 0

Printed in China.

Franklin Watts
An imprint of Hachette Children's Group
Part of The Watts Publishing Group
Carmelite House, 50 Victoria Embankment, London EC4Y 0DZ

An Hachette UK Company
ww.hachette.co.uk
www.franklinwatts.co.uk

MIX
Paper from responsible sources
FSC® C104740
www.fsc.org